THE INTERIOR MOUNTAIN

D1306106

Desert Saint

The
INTERIOR MOUNTAIN

*Encountering God
with the Desert Saints*

With Introductory Notes and Illustrations by
SIMON PETER IREDALE

ABINGDON PRESS
NASHVILLE

THE INTERIOR MOUNTAIN: ENCOUNTERING GOD WITH THE DESERT SAINTS

Copyright © 2000 by Abingdon Press

All rights reserved.
No part of this work may be reproduced or transmitted in any form or by any means, electronic or mechanical, including photocopying and recording, or by any information storage or retrieval system, except as may be expressly permitted by the 1976 Copyright Act or in writing from the publisher. Requests for permission should be addressed to Abingdon Press, P.O. Box 801, 201 Eighth Avenue South, Nashville, TN 37202-0801.

This book is printed on recycled, acid-free, elemental-chlorine-free paper.

Library of Congress Cataloging-in-Publication Data

Iredale, Simon, 1956–
   The Interior Mountain: encountering God with the desert saints: with introductory notes and illustrations / by Simon Iredale.
      p. cm.
   Includes bibliographical references(p.).
   ISBN 0-687-09022-9 (recycled, acid-free, elemental-chlorine-free paper)
      1. Desert Fathers—Quotations. 2. Spiritual life—Christianity—Quotations, maxims, etc.
   I. Title.

BR63 .I57 2000 99-046093
248.4'811 21—dc21   99-046093

Scripture quotations, unless otherwise noted, are from the New Revised Standard Version of the Bible. Copyright © 1989 by the Division of Christian Education of the National Council of the Churches of Christ in the United States of America. All rights reserved.

00 01 02 03 04 05 06 07 08—10 9 8 7 6 5 4 3 2 1

MANUFACTURED IN THE UNITED STATES OF AMERICA

About the Writer and Illustrator

Simon Peter Iredale is an ordained priest in the Church of England who works as a chaplain in the Royal Air Force. Educated at Cambridge University (M.Phil.), he did his theological training at Wycliffe Hall, Oxford, and the Ecumenical Institute, Bossey, Switzerland. He has had an enduring interest in Patristics and in the spirituality of Eastern Orthodox Christianity. He lived and taught for three years in Egypt, where he had the opportunity to visit the monastic sites in the Wadi El-Natrun where many of the desert saints lived. He has published many articles and poems. The illustrations included in this book were done using scraperboard, a technique by which the artist inscribes lines on a prepared black background.

Contents

Desert Monastery

INTRODUCTION
TO THE DESERT SAINTS

What is the Interior Mountain? Just as with Moses on Sinai, Elijah on Carmel, or the disciples on the mountain of the Transfiguration, it is the place of encounter with the living God. Where can the Interior Mountain be found? In its simplicity, its purity, its singleness of purpose in loving God, it can be found in every human heart. Through solitude and self-discipline, Antony of Egypt (circa *a.d.* 251–356) and the men and women who followed his pattern of life in the desert opened up new possibilities for our relationship with God.

Antony and his followers sought great solitude in the vast wilderness of the Egyptian desert and mountains living in cell-like huts and caves on a diet of water, hard bread, and whatever vegetables and herbs they could manage to grow. Solitaries and communities were also found in the Judean desert and, as in the case of Nilus and his son, on Mount Sinai. They devoted themselves entirely to prayer; silence; the study of Scripture; and simple physical work, weaving mats from palm fronds they exchanged for their meager supplies. As more monks joined them, they met for fellowship and the celebration of the Eucharist as frequently as they could; but their true homes remained their lonely cells.

It would be understandable if a modern reader were to ask at this stage, "What's the point? Shouldn't the Christian life be lived in the world?" The monks themselves would reply that they could better serve their fellow human beings by ceaselessly holding them in prayer than by engaging in much busyness and activity. In fact, their leaders were often consulted at times of crisis by the church; and they returned freely from the desert when there was a greater need. Antony himself returned to support the Christian martyrs in Alexandria during the persecution of 311–315, to help found the monastic communities of Scetis and Nitria, and to care for those suffering from the plague. The desert was not a retreat from the hostility of the world. The desert saints' attitude to spiritual warfare was utterly uncompromising. They saw Christian discipleship as a life-or-death battle with real, personal, evil powers. Although the desert saints knew the victory of Christ to be complete, they saw this life as a school of discipline in which God called each Christian to take up his or her cross and follow joyfully.

These are people who lived in the presence of God in a way that would be hard to parallel in our own distracted and superficial times. One is humbled by how much sheer dedication they brought to the study of Scripture; many of them knew the greater part of the Psalter by heart. While we feel that fifteen minutes of prayer is sufficient, they followed the apostle Paul's advice to pray at all times. Should we think that this must have led to a certain works-driven approach to worship, we are disarmed by their candor, wisdom, and psychological acuteness—the attitude of love and reverence that breathes from their sayings and prayers.

The value of their sayings to Christians like us as we enter a new millennium is enormous. It is hoped that this book will help many people discover an Interior Mountain within themselves; a place of encounter with God; a source of spiritual strength and consolation where, with a quiet heart, they might hear God's still, small voice. The sayings included in this book from this tradition were originally written in the early languages of the Near Eastern and Mediterranean world, in a time and culture that was not as conscious as we are today of how language can include some and exclude others. In addition, many of these sayings originated in communities that consisted mainly, although not exclusively, of men; so it made sense for them to talk mainly about "brothers" rather than about "brothers and sisters." In quoting the translations of these sayings (cited in the "Notes" section of this book), I have made an effort to use language inclusive of women and men in those sayings where doing so was helpful and appropriate. In other cases, I have retained less inclusive language to convey the sense and spirit of the original sayings or to avoid awkward sentence structures. With every saying I have tried to present the wisdom of the desert saints in contemporary English, avoiding words or turns of phrase not in common use today. It is also helpful to note that these sayings originated from both ammas and abbas. Therefore it is entirely accurate to talk about the "desert fathers and mothers." Communities of religious women existed from the very beginning, the sister of Pachomius being responsible for founding one of the first.

The eight themes chosen in the chapters that follow—Charity, Temptation, Self-Control, Stillness, Prayer, Simplicity, Solitude, and Endurance—draw out many of the ideas dear to the desert saints. We shall be approaching each theme in the form of a workshop where our own responses will form the main focus of the session. This is a study that can be done by oneself or with a group. But whether in solitude or in community, please bring with you your Bible, something to write with, and an expectant heart!

Practicing prayer and meditation like the desert saints is one way to help you to understand their spirituality. If you are sturying this book with a group or reading it alone, think about incorporating the prayers and Scripture sentences on pages 89–91 into your time with the desert saints. Use these prayers and Scripture sentences before or after each of the following chapters as you find most useful.

Monastic Egypt

MONASTIC EGYPT

Many of Antony's early followers were grouped in the area marked Cellia on the map (see page 12). In his time Alexandria was the see of one of the greatest theologians of the church, Bishop Athanasius. It had become rather too lively and overpopulated for the monks living just beyond its gates, so they traveled farther into the desert for the silence and solitude they required. Scetis and Nitria were early centers of common life communities, and famous monasteries are still flourishing in the former. These monasteries are now like stone ships on the ocean of the desert. Their very high walls were able to repulse the raiding Arab tribes of much later centuries. In the earlier period there must have been only the simplest cells for the monks, which they helped build for one another, rather like a monastic barn-raising!

As Antony's reputation spread (and this applied to many other of the abbas and ammas), he was forced to move to even more remote and wild places. The two monasteries named after him show roughly the area, in mountains between the valley of the Nile and the Red Sea, where he sought his Interior Mountain. Farther down river there were eventually large communities of religious people near the ancient site of Thebes. The monks sometimes used the ruins of an ancient Egyptian temple as a cell. A kind of monastic taxi in the form of a boat, which plied from the area of Tabennesis to Alexandria, kept the brothers and sisters in touch.

Charity

Chapter One

CHARITY

Abba Antony also said, "Our life and our death is with our neighbor. If we gain our neighbor, we have gained God, but if we scandalize our neighbor, we have sinned against Christ."[1]

Some monks of Scetis came one day to visit Amma Sarah. She offered them a small basket of fruit. They left the good fruit and ate the bad. So she said to them, "You are true monks of Scetis."[2]

A brother went to see an anchorite and as he was leaving said to him, "Forgive me, abba, for having taken you away from your rule." But the other answered him, "My rule is to refresh you and send you away in peace."[3]

An old man said, "Never have I wished to do something useful for myself which would harm my neighbor, for I have the firm hope that my neighbor's gain is a work full of fruit for me."[4]

One of the Fathers went off to the city to sell his manual work, and seeing a naked beggar he was moved by compassion and gave him his own habit. The poor man went and sold it. When he heard what he had done, the old man was very annoyed and repented of having given him the habit. That night Christ appeared to the old man in a dream; he was wearing the habit and said to him, "Do not grieve, for see I am wearing that which you have given me."[5]

An old man was asked, "What is humility?" He replied, "It is when someone sins against you and you forgive them before they come to ask for forgiveness."[6]

Some visitors came to the Thebaid one day to visit an old man, bringing one possessed with a devil that he might heal him. When they persistently asked him, the old man said to the devil, "Come out of God's creature." And the devil said to the old man, "I am going to come out, but I am going to ask you a question; tell me, who are the goats and who are the sheep?" The old man said, "I am one of the goats, but as for the sheep, God alone knows who they are." When he heard this the devil began to cry out with a loud voice, "Because of your humility, I am going away," and he departed at the same hour.[7]

One of the fathers used to say, "Every labor of the monk, without humility, is vain. For humility is the forerunner of love, as John was the forerunner of Jesus, drawing all people to him: even so humility draws to love, that is to God Himself, for God is love."[8]

A brother who had sinned was turned out of the church by the priest; Abba Bessarion got up and went with him, saying, "I, too, am a sinner."[9]

Abba John said, "We have put the light burden on one side, that is to say, self-accusation, and we have loaded ourselves with a heavy one, that is to say, self-justification."[10]

A soldier asked Abba Mius if God accepted repentance. After the old man had taught him many things he said, "Tell me, my dear, if your cloak is torn, do you throw it away?" He replied, "No, I mend it and use it again." The old man said to him, "If you are so careful about your cloak, will not God be equally careful about his creature?"[11]

Love in Action

For the desert saints, Christ's new commandment to love one another as he has loved us could not be an option or an ideal; it was a requirement of the Christian life. Similarly, they regarded Paul's image of the church as the body of Christ (1 Corinthians 12:12-31) as a demanding spiritual reality, not merely as an abstraction. The first saying sets out plainly, in Antony's usual direct style, the tremendous significance of our attitudes towards fellow human beings: "Our life and our death is with our neighbor." As we treat our neighbor, so the implication is, Christ will treat us. In the parable of the good Samaritan, our Lord has already shown us how large the scope of the term *neighbor* must be (Luke 10:29-37). We are not called only to love and serve Christ in the community of the church, but in our relationships with every human being.

The sayings reveal that the desert saints were people whose love was always turned towards others and away from their own wants and needs. Through constant prayer and concrete acts of kindness and hospitality, they engaged in a ministry to all humankind. At the heart of their "rule" was a commitment to engage in a profound ministry to whoever might cross their path. They did this without judgment, remembering that Christ came as the servant of all (Philippians 2:5-11). They understood that this extraordinary fact must mean that every person who follows him enters into the way of the servant. This is the way of salvation we have been shown, the holy way we have been called into for which pride and selfishness are anathema.

For the desert saints, the commandment to charity worked itself out in acts of hospitality and humility. Even though they had very little in their simple cells to offer a stranger, they would not hesitate to part with it in the name of Christ. Nothing was so important as the expression of care and love for the image of God standing before them in the form of a needy human being.

Hospitality is a fundamental part of the lives of the monks who still live in the monasteries of Wadi El-Natrun. If you were to visit one of these monasteries, you would be welcomed at the gate with gifts of bread and salt—symbols of the essentials of life. In addition, you would also be likely to receive strong sweet tea or coffee and the sticky cakes they delight to feed their guests. Something that impressed me greatly about the monasteries during my visits was the large number of young people who came out from Cairo to visit their spiritual mothers and fathers. For them the monasteries particularly kept an open door.

These desert saints also had a deep understanding of humility. We have often misunderstood this heavenly virtue. Our society teaches us to be self-publicists, go-getters, not shy to make our mark even in what can seem an overtly competitive way. We think of the world as a jungle in which only the aggressive will survive. We mistake humility for a kind of cravenness that allows others always to get their own way at our expense.

For the desert saints, however, humility was not a matter of low self-esteem or self-abasement. It was rooted in a profound understanding of the realities of our human nature, a wisdom that recognized our strengths and virtues but also our tragic weaknesses. It was a wisdom that knows that what is best about us springs solely from our relationship with Christ, understands that life itself is God's gift, and flees from the destructive effects of pride.

Such a sober understanding of what we are really like under the masks we love to wear can be a source of great strength. As the saying about John the Baptist, the forerunner of Jesus tells us, "humility is the forerunner of love." It is the prerequisite for a deeper experience of God's love. God will not come to persons whose pride leads them to believe that they are self-sufficient. The great and wise Abba Bessarion left the church with the brother who had sinned, not as an empty act of piety, a sort of spiritual "showing off," but because in his intense humility he understood that his need for God's love and forgiveness was just as great. Pride throws the desert sand in our own eyes; charity and humility give us, by God's grace, a strength that can overcome the world.

These sayings conclude with the heartwarming story of Abba Mius and the soldier. Underlying all our efforts to follow Christ is the overwhelming love of God that comes undeserved to every human being who seeks him. It makes me think also of the "torn cloak" of Christ's church. We have done so much damage to it over the centuries. We have stubbornly held to our divisions. We have so often been found wanting in charity and humility even towards the people of Christ's own household. Yet this "torn cloak" is still loved by God and will never be thrown away.

For Reflection

- We are used to thinking of charity in terms of how we use our money and possessions; but having read the excerpts from the sayings of the desert saints, is that the whole story?
- Antony said, "Our life and death is with our neighbor." What effect does this idea have on the way we see our fellow Christians? On the way we see those in the community around us? On the way we see the stranger or the enemy?
- The desert saints lived according to a simple "rule of life." Would there be advantages in drafting our own rule of life to monitor how we are living? What would your rule look like? Take the time to outline a rule for your own life, remembering that the vows in the monastic tradition had three primary emphases: simplicity, obedience, and self-control.
- What does humility mean to us in our aggressive and self-aggrandizing society? What is its relationship to charity?
- How does charity relate to our attitude toward creation, that is, to the world that surrounds us and its creatures?

Meditation on Charity

My hope is in the Father,
my refuge is the Son,
my shelter is the Holy Spirit.

O Holy Trinity,
Glory to Thee.
Glory to the Father,
and to the Son, and to the Holy Spirit,
both now, and ever
and unto ages of ages.
Amen.

The righteous shall answer
"Lord when did we see Thee
hungry and feed Thee,
or thirsty and give Thee drink?
And when did we see Thee
a stranger and welcome Thee,
or naked and clothe Thee?"
And the King will answer them,
"Truly, I say to you, as you did it
to one of the least of these
my brethren, you did it to me."

Lord, in the wilderness of this world
teach us to recognize your image
in the faces of our fellow human beings.
In our every word and action
may the surprise of the
kingdom of heaven be felt.

May we be worthy to hear
your words
"Come, O blessed of my Father."

Holy God
Holy Mighty
Holy Immortal
Have mercy upon us.

My hope is in the Father,
my refuge is the Son,
my shelter is the Holy Spirit.

Amen.

Temptation

Chapter Two

TEMPTATION

There was a monk who, because of the great number of his temptations, said, "I will go away from here." As he was putting on his sandals, he saw another man who was also putting on his sandals and this other monk said to him, "Is it on my account that you are going away? Because I go before you wherever you are going."[1]

Amma Theodora

The devil presents small sins to us as insignificant in our eyes, for otherwise he cannot lead us to great sins.[2]

Mark the Ascetic

There are eight principal thoughts, from which all other thoughts stem. The first thought is gluttony; the second, of fornication; the third, of love of money; the fourth, of discontent; the fifth, of anger; the sixth, of despondency; the seventh, of vainglory; the eighth, of pride. Whether these thoughts disturb the soul or not does not depend on us; but whether they linger in us or not and set passions in motion or not—does depend on us.[3]

Evagrius

Pray that temptation may not come upon you, but when it does come, accept it as something not alien but your own.[4]

Mark the Ascetic

In the end you will become worthy of God by the fact that you do nothing unworthy of him.[5]

Evagrius

An old man said, "Be like those who pass through the market place in front of an inn and breathe the smell of cooking and roasting. If they enjoy it, they go inside to eat some of it; if not, they only inhale the smell in passing and go on their way. It is the same for you: avoid the bad smell. Wake up and pray, saying, "Son of God, help me." Do this for other temptations also. For we do not have to uproot the passions, but resist them."[6]

If a temptation comes to you in the place where you live, do not leave the place at the time of temptation, for wherever you go you will find that which you fled from there before you. But stay until the temptation is past, that your departure may not cause offence and may be done in peace, and then you will not cause any distress amongst those who dwell in the place.[7]

An old man said, "For nine years a brother was tempted in thought to the point of despairing of his salvation, and being scrupulous he condemned himself, saying, 'I have lost my soul, and since I am lost I shall go back to the world.' But while he was on the way, a voice came to him on the road, which said, 'These nine years during which you have been tempted have been crowns for you; go back to your place, and I will allay these thoughts.' Understand that it is not good for people to despair of themselves because of their temptations; rather, temptations procure crowns for us if we use them well."[8]

A brother asked the abbot Pastor, saying, "I have sinned a great sin, and I am willing to do penance for three years." But the abbot Pastor said, "That is a lot!" And the brother said, "Do you order me penance for one year?" And again the old man said, "That is a lot!" Some who stood by said, "Up to forty days?" The old man said, "That is a lot!" And then he added, "I think that if someone would repent with their whole heart and would not reckon to do again that for which they now repent, God would accept a penance of three days."[9]

The abbot Macarius said, "If we dwell upon the harm that has been done to us by others, we cut off from our mind the power of dwelling upon God."[10]

Fighting Temptation

The desert saints saw human life, especially the life of the Christian, as the field of conflict for the spiritual battle. Their example for this was Christ's forty-day temptation by Satan in the wilderness (Mark 1:13). They took their ascetic training through prayer and self-denial just as seriously as any soldier would take preparation for war. A great part of this battle was recognizing, understanding, and resisting temptation. The desert saints certainly believed in personal evil powers or demons that were constantly attempting to ruin and distort the Christian's approach to God. Whatever we might make of this today, in a sense it does not matter what the source of temptation might be (whether it comes "from inside" or "from outside"). What matters is the belief that temptation is something real that has the potential of spoiling our relationship with Christ and with others. Hundreds of years before the development of psychology, the desert saints had a deep insight into the way our thoughts and feelings work. They recognized that there is a certain process through which temptations run. It starts with a simple thought, a suggestion that, as the saying from Evagrius makes clear, is blameless. We are free to choose to do good or evil; we have the potential for both. Problems start when we assent to this first suggestion. We accept the invitation offered by temptation, allowing the thought to grow. If this is allowed to continue, so the desert saints would say, it is only a matter of time before we act on the temptation.

Take the example of resentment. It occurs to us that we do not like a particular person. We hang on to the idea, letting it grow and develop, perhaps imagining situations where we say something cruel and clever to him or her. We imagine getting back at the person in some way for something he or she has done to us. Perhaps we brood on this for quite a while. This already is assenting to temptation. We recall what Jesus told us quite plainly about these angry feelings (Matthew 5:21-26). Perhaps then we get the opportunity to say or do something to that person to express our resentment. As we do, we stray further from the commandment of God; we lose another battle in the spiritual war.

Mark the Ascetic spoke of the way the devil uses small sins to lead us into greater ones, or, as we say in England, he uses "a sprat to catch a mackerel." We are particularly good at excusing our own behavior, often accepting in ourselves what we would condemn in another. Somehow it is always right for us; there are always mitigating circumstances. Both Christ and Paul spoke of a hardening of the heart, a spiritual process by which we develop habits of sin. We feel less and less that what we do is wrong. Indeed, after a while we do not even see the danger as a danger; and, once again, we lose another battle in the spiritual war.

The desert saints spoke also of the fact that temptation is something we cannot avoid, something that is, so to speak, tailor-made to us as people. We cannot move away from it because it comes with us and goes before us. Even in complete solitude in the middle of the desert, temptation is present. Mark also taught of the way memory can be used against us. Memories from the life we lived before we turned to Christ are used to try to draw us back into bad old habits, to undo the work of the Holy Spirit in us should that be possible. The desert saints well understood the need for a "healing of the memory."

So, are we sent into this battle without weapons with which to fight? Indeed we are not. The desert saints taught time and again of the way we have *made ourselves* vulnerable because we have not used the defense God has provided: the whole armor of God. First in this heavenly defense is prayer. The desert saints used the Jesus Prayer ("Lord Jesus Christ, Son of God, have mercy upon me, a sinner.") and the Lord's Prayer at times of temptation. These are direct appeals to God to act, and they are not made in vain. Second is the defense of Scripture. The desert saints spent a great deal of their time in psalmody, turning their hearts and minds to God. Third, there is the whole aspect of what later teachers called "avoiding the occasion of sin." If you know there is some place or activity that will make you vulnerable to temptation, avoid it; do not allow the process of temptation even to start.

Added to all this is what the desert saints called "guarding the door of the heart." Be aware of what is going on in you, and keep watch on your thoughts. Be mindful of where they seek to take you.

You may feel that this is an impossible task. The desert saints did not pretend that the way of discipleship is easy, but the reward of knowing God in Christ eclipses any effort we have contributed ourselves. We can be reassured by the thought that we are only tempted so fiercely *because* we are trying to follow Christ. "Temptations procure crowns," reads one of the desert sayings in this chapter. What does that mean? Here we have an indication of the wisdom and power of God. Although God tempts no one (James 1:13), the desert saints understood that even the testing of temptation works for our spiritual benefit and growth. How do athletes grow stronger and fitter? By trying their strength against the competition, perhaps losing many times before they begin to win. Remember that God does not permit you to be tempted beyond your strength

(1 Corinthians 10:13) and that no part of our lives is beyond the reach of God's power and love. Out of the testing fires of temptation, the gold of a faithful life shines most brightly.

For Reflection

- How do you understand temptation yourself? Do you see it as something "coming from outside," an attack that should be resisted? Do you see it as "coming from inside," primarily in terms of our own psychology, our own weakness and imperfections? What do you make of the desert saints' view of how temptation "works"?
- One of the monks says that "temptations procure crowns for us." What does this statement mean to you? What are the "benefits" of experiencing temptation?
- The desert saints and Jesus evidently believed in the activity and hostility of demons. Evil spirits were thought to oppose and subvert a person's decision to love and obey God. What do you think about demons?
- What are the weapons of the Spirit that we can employ against temptation? Are there also practical ways to defend ourselves? What seemed to work for the saints in these sayings?
- How do you make sense of evil? Do you see it as an external, personal force, a possibility to you in your everyday life? Or is it just a matter of bad people, bad decisions, and indifference to the sufferings of others?

Meditation on Temptation

My hope is in the Father,
my refuge is the Son,
my shelter is the Holy Spirit.

O Holy Trinity,
Glory to Thee.
Glory to the Father, and to the Son,
and to the Holy Spirit,
both now, and ever,
and unto ages of ages.
Amen.

Defend us, O Lord
from evil within and without.
By the power of your Cross
by which you ransomed our lives;
by the power of your resurrection
by which you overcame death
and burst the gloomy gates of hell;
defend us, O Lord.

You shared our human life
and know our weakness;
your cosmos-compelling love anticipates
the feeble motions of
our own love for you.

In your forgiveness
you call us a new creation;
give us strength to live as

children of light
in an often dark and tragic world.
In the midst of temptation
be our strong tower,
our high and holy place,
our peace.

Holy God
Holy Mighty
Holy Immortal
Have mercy upon us.

My hope is in the Father,
my refuge is the Son,
my shelter is the Holy Spirit.
Amen.

Self-Control

Chapter Three

SELF-CONTROL

Certain brothers were sitting near Abba Poemen and one brother began praising another, saying, "That brother is a good man, for he hates evil." The old man said, "And what is it, to hate evil?" The brother didn't know how to answer, and himself asked, "Tell me, Abba, what is it to hate evil?" And the old man said, "The person who hates evil, hates their own sins, and blesses and loves every one of their brothers."[1]

A devout person happened to be insulted by someone, and replied, "I could say as much to you, but the commandment of God keeps my mouth shut."[2]

Amma Theodora

Someone begged an old man to accept some money for his needs, but he refused, saying that his manual work supplied all that was necessary. When the other insisted that he should accept at least enough for his essential needs, the old man replied, "It would be a double shame to accept it: for me to receive what I do not need, and for you to give me what belongs to others."[3]

Two old men had lived together for many years and had never fought with one another. The first said to the other, "Let us also have a fight like other men do." The other replied, "I do not know how to fight." The first said to him, "Look, I will put a brick between us, and I will say it is mine, and you say, 'No, it is mine,' and so the fight will begin." So they put a brick between them and the first said,

33

"This brick is mine," and the other said, "No, it is mine," and the first responded, "If it is yours, take it and go"—so they gave it up without being able to find an occasion for argument.[4]

It is good not to get angry, but if this should happen, the Apostle does not allow you a whole day for this passion, for he says: "Let not the sun go down" (Ephesians 4.26). Will you wait till all your time is ended? Why hate the person who has grieved you? It is not they who have done the wrong, but the devil. Hate sickness but not the sick person.[5]

Amma Syncletica

A monk met the handmaids of God upon a certain road, and at the sight of them he turned out of the way. And the abbess said to him, "If you had been a perfect monk, you would not have looked so close as to notice that we were women."[6]

The abbot Agatho said, "If an angry person were to raise the dead, because of their anger they would not please God."[7]

The old men used to say that the temptation to lust is like a hook. If it is suggested to us and we do not let ourselves be overcome by it, it is easily cut off; but if, once it is presented, we take pleasure in it and let ourselves be overcome, it transforms itself and becomes like iron and is difficult to cut off. Thus discernment is needed about these thoughts, because for those who allow themselves to be seduced there is no hope of salvation, whereas crowns are prepared for the others.[8]

An old man said, "The person who is honored and praised more than they deserve suffers great harm thereby, whereas one who is not honored by others at all will be glorified above."[9]

One of the old men went to another old man one day, and while they were speaking, the first said, "I am dead to the world." The other old man said, "Do not count on it, brother, before you have left the body, for even if you say you are dead, yet Satan is not dead."[10]

Life in Community

Having pondered on the desert saints' understanding of temptation, it is very appropriate, in this chapter on self-control, for us to consider our relationships with others. Both solitude and community, as opposite poles of the same spiritual endeavor, defined the desert life. One of the stories in this chapter seems quite amusing, that of the two old men who had never had a quarrel; but what is expressed here is the kind of communion between human beings, and between human beings and God, that is the goal of the Christian life.

Underlying the idea of community in these writings was the developing theology of the Holy Trinity. The great teachers of the Eastern Church (Basil, Gregory of Nyssa, and Gregory Nazianzus) were at this time drawing together an understanding of the Christian life as a participation through Christ in the divine life of the Holy Trinity. That sounds rather complicated; but if we think of Christ's promise that we are "born again" (John 3:3), it begins to make more sense. When we turn to Christ, it is far more than just a change on the surface (in the way we live or in our habits and opinions). It is a change as complete as a new birth. The life we lead from then on, though it is similar to the old in many outward appearances, is really a new life given to us by God. The old has gone completely; the new creation (2 Corinthians 5:17) will last forever. This is Christ's gift to us of his own resurrection life. As Paul noted, it is Christ living in us (Galatians 2:20).

The community of the church becomes not just a convenient collection of people who believe the same things, but a community of salvation, quite literally, a foretaste of heaven. Does your church feel like a foretaste of heaven? Perhaps not! But every church where the name of Christ is honored is a part of Christ's church, and God will keep his promises. The church should strive to reflect the perfect communion of the three Persons of the Trinity, and the quality of the relationships we have with one another is the cornerstone of that community. Through humility, self-control, and charity, community becomes the supreme place where we encounter God. For this reason, the saints were particularly fierce about anger and lust, both of which destroy proper human relationships within community.

We have seen already how Christ teaches that anger can be a kind of murder in the heart. At the same time, the desert saints (with the apostle Paul in Ephesians 4:26) accepted that losing one's temper is the lot of every human being. Again, rather like temptation, a great deal depends on what happens *next*. If we offer a cruel word, malicious gossip, or an aggressive action, then we join and reinforce the cycle of bitterness. I am sure we have seen how destructive this can be in communities other than the church. Amma Syncletica tells us to identify the root of the evil (not the person, but evil itself: "Hate sickness but not the sick person."). The root of anger is frequently a false idea of self, hurt pride, or the frustration of desire.

What is particularly sinister about both anger and lust is that they change our perceptions of the other person in a way that dehumanizes her or him. In the case of anger, the person can become a "hate object." We do not allow this person to be just like us, a mixture of good and bad. He or she becomes entirely bad, entirely deserving of our anger. At that moment we forget that Christ loves this person and died for him or her too. We do not think that this person has been created in the image of God. If we did, the anger would pass.

There are many sayings about the damaging effects of lust—not, it must be noted, because the desert saints necessarily saw our sexual drives as evil or unnatural. Many sayings advised the young monk to keep well out of the way of temptation; but these sayings were primarily intended for those seeking to follow the monastic life, which is, by definition, celibate. We have already seen how temptation can use the experiences of life, and our memories of them, as enticements to sin. For our purposes, what is important is the way lust turns the other person into an object of selfish desire, a "thing" to be used for pleasure. This is dehumanizing, since the thoughts, the needs, and the uniqueness of the person are not considered. Both anger and lust break communion between people, for in both cases we effectively make the other less than a person. When we do this, we also break our communion with God and grieve the Holy Spirit (Ephesians 4:30).

For Reflection

- The desert saints saw anger arising out of wounded pride, frustrated desire, or a false idea of self. What are the things that make you angry?
- If we shall be required to give account of every word that we utter (Matthew 12:36-37), how can we be more mindful of how we speak, of what we say, and of how much we are willing to listen?
- It would be unrealistic to think that people will never "fall out" with one another, but how could conflict be seen as creative? What seemed to work for the desert saints? Think of a conflict you have experienced with another person. How could the principles of the desert tradition have helped you?

Meditation on Self-Control

My hope is in the Father,
my refuge is the Son,
my shelter is the Holy Spirit.

O Holy Trinity,
Glory to Thee.
Glory to the Father, and to the Son,
and to the Holy Spirit,
both now, and ever
and unto ages of ages.
Amen.

Our passions shake us like
a tree in a high wind.
O Lord whose word calmed
the raging sea, calm
our troubled hearts.

Resentment is a poison, anger
a fever, and we are like
a sick man who will not
own his sickness.
O Lord whose love heals the
deepest wounds,
touch our wounded hearts.

Harsh words once spoken
cannot be recalled.
O Word of God sent
for our salvation, set

a watch on our lips so each
word serves to build up, not
to destroy.

Holy God
Holy Mighty
Holy Immortal
Have mercy upon us.

My hope is in the Father,
my refuge is the Son,
my shelter is the Holy Spirit.

Amen.

Stillness

Chapter Four

STILLNESS

Do you desire, then, to embrace this life of solitude, and to seek out the blessings of stillness? If so, abandon the cares of the world, and the principalities and powers that lie behind them; free yourself from attachment to material things, from domination by passions and desires, so that as a stranger to all this you may attain true stillness.[1]

Evagrius

Be like an astute businessman: make stillness your criterion for testing the value of everything, and choose always what contributes to it.[2]

Evagrius

It was said that there were three friends who were not afraid of hard work. The first chose to reconcile those who were fighting each other, as it is said, "Blessed are the peace-makers." (Matthew 5.) The second chose to visit the sick. The third went to live in prayer and stillness in the desert. Now in spite of all his labors, the first could not make peace in all people's quarrels; and in his sorrow he went to him who was serving the sick, and he found him also disheartened, for he could not fulfill that commandment either. So they went together to see him who was living in the stillness of prayer. They told him their difficulties and begged him to tell them what to do. After a short silence, he poured some water into a bowl and said to them, "Look at the water," and it was disturbed. After a little while he said to them again, "Look how still the water is now," and as they looked into the water, they saw their own faces reflected in it as in a mirror. Then he said to them, "It is the same for those who live among others; disturbances prevent them from seeing their faults. But when you are still, especially in the desert, then you see your failings."[3]

A brother came to see a very experienced old man and said to him, "I am in trouble," and the old man said to him, "Sit in your cell and God will give you peace."[4]

Abba Poemen said, "Do not give your heart to that which does not satisfy your heart."[5]

Abba Sisoes said, "Seek God, and do not seek where he dwells."[6]

It was said of Abba Agathon that for three years he lived with a stone in his mouth, until he learned to be silent.[7]

Abba Poemen said, "You may seem to be silent, but if your heart is condemning others, you are babbling ceaselessly. But there may be another who talks from morning till night and yet is truly silent; that is, he says nothing that is not profitable."[8]

A brother questioned a young monk, saying, "Is it better to be silent or to speak?" The young man said to him, "If the words are useless, leave them alone, but if they are good, give place to the good and speak. Furthermore, even if they are good, do not prolong speech, but terminate it quickly, and you will have peace, quiet, rest."[9]

If a jar of wine is left in the same place for a long time, the wine in it becomes clear, settled and fragrant. But if it is moved about, the wine becomes turbid and dull, tainted throughout by the lees. So you, too, should stay in the same place and you will find how greatly this benefits you.[10]

Evagrius

Silence in the Spirit

Stillness and silence, both translations of the Greek word *hesychia,* were very important to the desert saints. What is meant is not inactivity or merely outward silence, for the saying from Abba Poemen reveals that such outward silence can mask a veritable storm of thoughts: "A person may seem to be silent, but if their heart is condemning others, they are babbling ceaselessly." In these terms, anyone can be "silent" without it having any spiritual value at all. The stillness of the desert saints was more like a special kind of listening in which they attentively waited upon God. The saints spoke of the way one can gradually turn away, in this stillness, from the distractions of the senses and of memory. By keeping the heart fixed on God, often by the occasional gentle repetition of the Jesus Prayer (see page 89), we can find that place of stillness in us that is the spring of our spiritual life.

Evagrius with his image of the lees clouding the wine reminds us of how activity for its own sake can be a positive disadvantage to the spiritual life. The feeling of many Christians today is that if they are not actively "doing something" for the church or for God, if their diaries are not full to overflowing, then something must be wrong. Sometimes it may be that God would like us to sit down and listen so that our activity could then be directed aright. The story about the three friends is very helpful here. The friends who go out into the world go for the best possible reasons. However, because they rely on their own strength and do not seek first that profound communion with God that can be found through stillness, their efforts just wear them out. It is as if we know that we must run a race but set out in every direction that takes our fancy until exhausted we think to ask, "In which direction would you like me to run?"

Stillness is the cultivation of an attitude of the heart. In John's Gospel we hear that Jesus leaves his peace with us (John 14:27), but how much do we actually experience this peace? It is obviously not just like the quietness that follows noise or the tranquillity of the countryside, for it is a peace that passes understanding. It is the peace of the martyrs that sustained them in their hour of witness. It is the peace that can be experienced in the uproar of a city. The stillness of the desert saints, which is an experience of Christ's peace, places us in the presence of the one who says, "Be still, and know that I am God!" (Psalm 46:10).

Stillness is also an opportunity for healing. Take the advice of the old man to the person who was in trouble: "Sit in your cell and God will give you peace." That might strike us as very strange, perhaps even as rather harsh. However, more than anything else it is a pointer to that communion with God that stillness seeks. Do we not believe that God knows what our problem is? Do we feel we must solve it without his help? When it comes right down to it, don't we think he loves us enough to help us with our problem? Do we commit a problem to God and then anxiously snatch it back? The desert saints echoed the New Testament when it insisted, "Cast all your anxiety on him [God], because he cares for you" (1 Peter 5:7). Didn't Christ himself tell us not to be anxious (Matthew 6:25-34)? The old man simply told this troubled person to trust God's promise, to trust his love.

The remarkable example of Abba Agathon, who kept a stone in his mouth for three years until he learned to be silent, reminds us that even when there *was* something worth saying, something that rose above idle chatter, the desert saints treated the tongue with the wariness James recommended (James 3:1-12). The theme of "guarding of the heart" and of stillness must also include the guarding of the tongue. Many of the desert sayings were directed towards the harm that gossip and spiteful talk can do to community. However, we tend to think that mere talk does not matter. The desert saints recalled what Jesus said about the things that defile a person being those that come from within, out of the heart (Mark 7:14-23). They also recalled the solemn and terrible promise of the

Lord that all human beings will have to give account for every care-less word they speak (Matthew 12:36). As a general principle we could say, "Would I say this thing about a person if the person were here?" or, "Everything I say is in the presence of Christ; shall I say this hurtful thing?" The desert saint replied that even if your words are good, "do not prolong speech, but terminate it quickly, and you will have peace, quiet, rest."

For Reflection

- Think of an occasion when you have had a problem and prayed for God's help. Were you able to let God handle it, or did you continue to worry about it? What happened? What did that teach you about God?
- One can become addicted to activity that is just a mask for rest-lessness. Think about the things you do that do not really bring rest and comfort to your life. What are they? Which of these can you give up? Could you achieve more by being still?
- Through the media and now the Internet, our lives are increas-ingly saturated with information and distractions we could probably live without. Could you practice more discipline in how much time and attention you give to these things?
- Given the noise and stress of modern life, how can you create a place of stillness where you can regularly listen to God? What makes silence and solitude difficult in your life? Which of these difficulties are within your ability to change? Which are not?

Meditation on Stillness

My hope is in the Father,
my refuge is the Son,
my shelter is the Holy Spirit.

O Holy Trinity,
Glory to Thee.
Glory to the Father, and to the Son,
and to the Holy Spirit,
both now, and ever
and unto ages of ages.
Amen.

In the broken mirror of our hearts,
all things but your face,
O Lord, are reflected.
Looking into your face may
we see you as you truly are,
and ourselves as your children.

Like a startled flock of birds our
thoughts fly off in
every direction.
Lord, may they all return in
peace to nest in
your truth.

Holy God
Holy Mighty
Holy Immortal
Have mercy upon us.

My hope is in the Father,
my refuge is the Son,
my shelter is the Holy Spirit.

Amen.

Prayer

Chapter Five

PRAYER

They told of Abba Arsenius that on Saturday evening with the Sabbath drawing on, he would leave the sun behind him and stretching out his hands towards heaven, would pray until, with the morning of the Sabbath, the rising sun shone upon his face. So he would stay.[1]

They asked Abba Macarius, "How ought we to pray?" and the old man said, "There is no need of much speaking in prayer, but often stretch out your hands and say, 'Lord, as you will and as you know, have mercy upon me.' But if there is war in your soul, add, 'Help me.' And because He knows what we need, He shows us mercy."[2]

Stand patiently and pray steadfastly, brushing off the impacts of worldly cares and all thoughts; for they distract and worry you in order to disturb the impetus of your prayer.[3]

Nilus of Sinai

Prayer is a branch (of the tree) of meekness, and freedom from anger.
Prayer is an expression of joy and thankfulness.
Prayer is a remedy against sorrow and depression.[4]

Nilus of Sinai

Those who collect in themselves distress and resentment and who practice prayer in this state are like someone pouring water into a leaky bucket.[5]

Nilus of Sinai

49

Having prayed as is fitting, expect what is unfitting, and stand firm, protecting your fruit. This has been your task from the very beginning—to cultivate and keep (Genesis 2:15). Therefore having cultivated (having prayed as you ought), do not leave unprotected the fruits of your labor, or no profit will be left from your prayer.[6]

Nilus of Sinai

The one who prays with understanding patiently accepts circumstances, whereas the one who resents them has not yet attained pure prayer.[7]

Mark the Ascetic

The whole warfare between us and the unclean spirits is for the sake of spiritual prayer; for to them it is most harmful and unbearable and to us salutary and favorable.[8]

Nilus of Sinai

The Holy Spirit, in compassion for our weakness, comes to us even when we are still impure; and if only he finds our mind sincerely praying to him, descends upon it and disperses all the swarms of thoughts and images which surround it, thus disposing it towards desire for spiritual prayer.[9]

Nilus of Sinai

A brother said to Abba Antony, "Pray for me." The old man said to him, "I will have no mercy upon you, nor will God have any, if you yourself do not make an effort and if you do not pray to God."[10]

At the times when you remember God, increase your prayers, so that when you forget Him, the Lord may remind you.[11]

Mark the Ascetic

The Language of Love

How would it be if you said that you loved someone and that person was always with you, but you spoke to him or her for only five minutes every day? How would it be if you had the wisest person possible ready to help and guide you, but you hardly ever asked him or her a question? Prayer is the language of love to our heavenly Father who hears in secret (Matthew 6:6). Prayer is the source of all wisdom and comfort from the one called the Comforter. Prayer is the moment when we know ourselves most truly as God's children who have the right, bought so dearly, to say "Abba," Father, to the creator of all things.

Even though we may know all this, we still find it hard to make time to pray. The world crowds in with other responsibilities that appear perfectly genuine and reasonable. Yet as a modern "spiritual mother" once said to me, "How can you expect to feed others when you do not eat yourself?" Antony had little patience with our excuses: "I will have no mercy on you, nor will God have any, if you yourself do not make an effort and if you do not pray to God."

Perhaps we need to have a broader idea of prayer. As with any relationship, the one we have with God changes and deepens as we live with him. There are times when we *do* need to talk long and earnestly with God, bringing before him the things on our heart. At other times, we can rest in his presence silently. Many people made long and arduous journeys to ask the desert saints how to pray. Their answers show us that prayer is not so much something we do as it is a life that we live. There are as many different ways to pray as there are people. This makes perfect sense, for God has called each one of us to be a unique person in Christ. Since this is true, how could there be only one way to pray? However, there are some common features.

We must not bring resentment or selfish motives into prayer, becoming like the "leaky bucket" Nilus describes. Jesus also teaches us to make our peace with others before we come to prayer (Matthew 5:23-24). We do not need to tell God anything about our needs, as if he does not know already. Too much talk and not enough listening can make prayer barren. What a tremendous relief it is to know that we do not need to pray only on our "good" days when we imagine we are "presentable" before God. Nilus speaks of the compassion of the Holy Spirit who comes to us even when we are in a mess.

The desert saints understood that prayer is a great gift of God active in us. God takes the initiative. God moves us to pray; calls us to him; and, through the groanings of the Holy Spirit (Romans 8:26), gives us words for feelings we cannot, in our weakness, find words for. Prayer does not need to be eloquent. The educated pray no better than those of little learning. The great saint Antony may have had no formal education, yet bishops and princes came to ask his advice. Prayer does not require a special language; before God, only honesty and sincerity of heart count. Macarius reminds us of the utter simplicity of the praying heart when he says, "Lord, as you will, as you know, have mercy on me." And in times of trouble add, "Help me." What could be simpler than that? What could be more honest? We learn from the sayings how turning our hearts and minds frequently to God requires patience and resistance to the buffeting of thoughts that would distract us; we learn also that it is the greatest defense against evil.

What did Nilus mean by, "Having prayed as is fitting, expect what is unfitting, and stand firm, protecting your fruit"? The saints believed in the reality of the spiritual battle where the Christian sometimes could be besieged by the forces of evil. At these moments, only prayer, calling on the name of the Lord, would serve to defend them. Indeed, as Nilus said in another situation, the very fact that we have this extraordinary access to God brings this fierce conflict upon us. Without being too dramatic about it, we can say that there are certainly times in every Christian's life when we feel overshadowed by something hostile. We often can find no words for these feelings of dread or depression; but it is the sure experience of the whole church, including the desert saints, that calling upon the name of the Lord is our first and best response. For reasons that are beyond our understanding, we are particularly conscious of this opposition when we make genuine progress in the Christian life. "Guarding our fruit" in this context is not allowing our progress towards a deeper life with Christ to be hindered. When we pray, we surround ourselves with the powers of heaven and claim Christ's victory in the very midst of our weakness and temptation.

For Reflection

- The desert saints talk about prayer distraction. What do you think they mean by this? What distractions do you face in prayer? How did the saints deal with these distractions? What might work for you?
- The desert saints understood that prayer was sometimes a time of struggle and striving rather than a time of refreshment and comfort. Is prayer ever a struggle for you? If so, in what ways?
- What do you think is the purpose of prayer? If God knows, better than we, what we need before we ask, what are we seeking to do in prayer? Is prayer something we do or something we become?
- According to the desert saints, prayer is our greatest weapon in the spiritual conflict. What is your prayer life actually like? How can prayer be a more important part of your life? What are you willing to give up so that you can pray more?

Meditation on Prayer

My hope is in the Father,
my refuge is the Son,
my shelter is the Holy Spirit.

O Holy Trinity,
Glory to Thee.
Glory to the Father, and to the Son,
and to the Holy Spirit,
both now, and ever
and unto ages of ages.
Amen.

"In the midst of the lamp-stands
one like a son of man,
his eyes were like a flame of fire,
his feet were like burnished bronze,
refined as in a furnace, and his voice
was like the sound of many waters;
and his face was like the
sun in full brightness."

To you Lord
terrible in your beauty
we dare to pray,
and yet you are closer
to us than this
next breath we take.
Your Spirit, love-bearer,
groans in us with groans
too deep for words.

Prayer

Like a leaping mountain stream
let our prayers pierce,
dance over and sweep away
all that keeps us back from
knowing and loving
you more truly.

May our prayer be your
life beating within us.

Holy God
Holy Mighty
Holy Immortal
have mercy upon us.

My hope is in the Father,
my refuge is the Son,
my shelter is the Holy Spirit.

Amen.

Simplicity

Chapter Six

SIMPLICITY

God sells righteousness at a very low price to those who wish to buy it: a little piece of bread, a cloak of no value, a cup of cold water, a small coin.[1]

Some thieves once came into an old man's cell, and said to him, "Whatever you have in your cell, we have come to take away." And he said, "Take whatever you see, my sons." So they took whatever they could find in the cell, and went away. But they forgot a little bag that was hidden in the cell. So the old man, picking it up, followed after them, shouting and saying, "My sons, you forgot this: take it." But they, amazed at the old man's patience, brought everything back to his cell, and they all asked for forgiveness, saying to each another, "This really is a man of God."[2]

It was asked of Syncletica of blessed memory if to have nothing is a perfect good. And she said, "It is a great good for those who are able. For those who can endure it endure suffering in their bodies, but they have quiet of soul. Even as stout garments trodden underfoot and turned over in the washing are made clean and white, so is a strong soul made steadfast by voluntary poverty."[3]

Someone brought an old man money, saying, "Spend this money on yourself, for you are old and sick." He was indeed a leper. But the old man said, "Have you come to take away my Shepherd after sixty years? During the many years of my sickness I have not lacked anything; God has cared for me and fed me." And he refused to take it.[4]

Abba Pambo asked Abba Antony, "What ought I to do?" and the old man said to him, "Do not trust in your own righteousness, do not worry about the past, but control your tongue and your stomach."[5]

Abba Isaiah said that Abba Pambo used to say, "The monk should wear a garment of such a kind that he could throw it out of his cell for three days and no-one would steal it."[6]

A brother asked Abba Tithoes, "How should I guard my heart?" The old man said to him, "How can we guard our hearts when our mouths and our stomachs are open?"[7]

A brother said to Abba Poemen, "Give me a word," and he said to him, "As long as the pot is on the fire, no fly nor any other animal can get near it, but as soon as it is cold, these creatures get inside. So it is for the monk: as long as he lives in spiritual activities, the enemy cannot find a means of overthrowing him."[8]

Choose the meekness of Moses and you will find your heart which is a rock changed into a spring of water.[9]

Amma Syncletica

The more we use moderation in our lives, the more we are at peace, for we are not full of cares for many things—servants, hired laborers and acquisition of cattle. But when we cling to such things, we become liable to vexations arising from them and are led to murmur against God. Thus our self-willed desire (for many things) fills us with turmoil and we wander in the darkness of a sinful life, not knowing ourselves.[10]

Abba Antony

When someone asked Abba Isaiah what avarice was, he replied, "Not to believe that God cares for you, to despair of the promises of God and to love boasting."[11]

Voluntary Poverty

If you were to enter the cell of a desert saint, you would be forgiven for thinking that no one lived there at all. You would perhaps find the simplest bowl of rough pottery for food and maybe a jar for water propped up against the wall. It is unlikely that there would be anything like furniture. As to changes of clothes, we have Abba Pambo's opinion on that: "The monk's garment should be such that he could throw it out of his cell for three days and no-one would take it." We are reminded of Jesus' instructions to the Twelve: "Take nothing for your journey, no staff, nor bag, nor bread, nor money—not even an extra tunic" (Luke 9:3). Just as a soldier's equipment is limited to what is absolutely essential for the battle, so in preparation for the spiritual battle we are to discard as useless many of the things we might consider essential to our lives.

Possessions in themselves are not evil. Christ taught that the desire for material things, the distorted attitudes of the heart, created, at best, an obstacle to our knowing God. At worst, this drive to possess could become a form of idolatry. We remember the story of the rich ruler (Luke 18:18-27) who, because of his attachment to his possessions, could not become a disciple. It is this deep attachment to possessions, the "need to have," that seems to make discerning the things of the kingdom of God that much harder. How hard is indicated by Jesus' image of the camel going through the eye of a needle. Athanasius in his *Life of Antony* says that the young Antony heard this story read one morning in church, and it inspired him to give away all his possessions and to make his first great step towards the life of the desert. The desert saints set out to break this attachment to possessions in the most radical way possible. They pared down the things that supported life—food, drink, and shelter—to levels below what we would consider possible. They did not even allow old age or infirmity to deflect them for an instant from the rigor of their rule. Even the old man suffering from leprosy refused to accept money to alleviate his suffering. This is not just plain awkwardness, as his reply tells us: "Have you come to take away my Shepherd after sixty years? During the many years of my sickness I have not lacked anything; God has cared for me and fed me." Here he is referring directly to the Lord's promise (Matthew 6:25-34) to care for our physical as well as our spiritual needs. Perhaps we would be surprised that someone would take these words as a program for life. Could anyone actually live like that? The desert saints obviously thought so.

We need to be very aware that the poverty the saints pursued was one they had freely chosen as a sign of the Kingdom in the world. They would not regard involuntary poverty, where people are deprived of the basics of life without their choice, as anything but an evil. Indeed, they would probably understand such poverty as being one of the tragic results of sin, greed or lack of charity among others. Abba Isaiah saw avarice as a terrible kind of unbelief. It is the equivalent to not believing that God cares for you, despairing of the promises of God, and hating one's neighbor. From this we see that fussing about possessions, whether we have something or not, is to miss the point completely. It is the underlying spiritual attitudes that are crucial. One could imagine that even if the desert saints were suddenly overwhelmed with riches, they would be completely indifferent to them. There is the amusing, and moving, story of the old man visited by thieves who runs after them shouting, "You forgot this: take it." These treasures which "moth and rust consume and where thieves break in and steal" (Matthew 6:19) are worth less than nothing compared to the riches of heaven that can never be taken away.

The desert saints knew well, however, that simply having nothing did not heal the desire for material things. Greediness and self-ishness could shadow their lives even if it was only the question of eating a dried fig. Their radical approach to poverty meant that there would be much soul-searching over things that we would consider a very small concession to appetite. "It was said of an old man that one day he wanted a small fig. Taking one, he held it up in front of his eyes, and not being overcome by his desire, he repented, reproaching himself for even having had this wish."

Are we then to sell all we have and follow Christ in the way of the desert saints? Like Antony, that may well be what God is saying to us. If very many of us did this, it would certainly have a remarkable effect on our communities! Even if we do not, like them, use our voluntary poverty as a sign of the Kingdom, it is certainly good to be reminded so powerfully about what is truly valuable in this world and what will pass away like a dream. Nothing really belongs to us in the end because we are mortal. The greatest possessions in the world will pass to another one day, and we can do nothing to hold them back. What is truly our own is what God offers us in Christ. He is "the pearl of great price" (Matthew 13:45-46) for which we sell all we have to possess forever.

For Reflection

- Are you sometimes more concerned about your outward appearance (what you wear, what you drive, or where you live) than about what your spiritual life looks like to God? Try to name three things you desire that may be impediments to your spiritual growth.
- God's promise to us is that he will supply us with what we truly

need (Matthew 6:25-33). Is our anxiety about material things a sign of little faith? For what material things are you anxious? What would it look like to have more faith about those things?

- Just as water always seeks the lowest level, so the desert saints' humility constantly sought to unite them with their lowliest brethren, with the outcast and the despised. In our competitive and divided societies how can we attempt to follow this Christlike path?
- Think of a time in your life when you may have had to go without food, shelter, or adequate clothing. Was it a voluntary or an involuntary deprivation? What was your reaction to this situation? What did you learn from it?

Meditation on Simplicity

My hope is in the Father,
my refuge is the Son,
my shelter is the Holy Spirit.

O Holy Trinity,
Glory to Thee.
Glory to the Father, and to the Son,
and to the Holy Spirit,
both now, and ever
and unto ages of ages.
Amen.

All good things come of Thee
bountiful Lord,
and of your own do we give Thee.

Simplicity

Of the things
we touch and taste and see,
nothing will remain;
of the things which lure and entangle
us in the love of possessions,
nothing will remain;
of the things which worry and upset us
which shadow our
lives with conflict,
nothing will remain.

Only your promises remain
O Fountainhead of life!
Only your love remains
O Eternal Lover!
Only your faithfulness remains
O Rock of Ages!

Lead us into the school
of your heavenly training.
Let your image shine forth
in each life lived
in the way of Christ.

Holy God
Holy Mighty
Holy Immortal
Have mercy upon us.

My hope is in the Father,
my refuge is the Son,
my shelter is the Holy Spirit.

Amen.

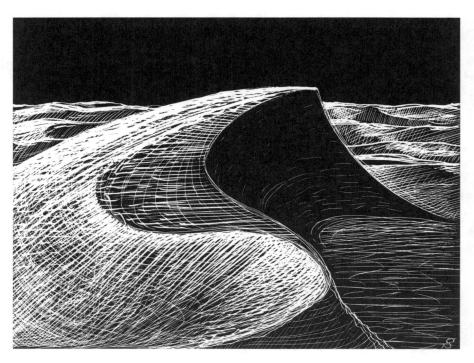

Solitude

Chapter Seven

SOLITUDE

Abba Antony said, "Fish, if they linger on dry land, die: even so monks that linger outside their cell or live with people of the world fall away from their vow of quiet. As a fish must return to the sea, so must we to our cell: otherwise through lingering outside, we might forget the watch within."[1]

At one time the judge of the province came to see the abbot Simon, and he took the leather girdle that he wore and climbed into the palm tree to prune it. And when they came up they said to him, "Where is the old man who inhabits this solitude?" And he answered, "There is no solitary here." And when he said this, the judge departed.[2]

A certain brother, having renounced the world and taken the habit, straightway shut himself up, saying, "I have decided to be a solitary." But when the older men of the neighborhood heard about it, they came and threw him out and made him go round the cells of the brothers and do penance before each saying, "Forgive me, for I am not a solitary, but have only now attempted to begin to be a monk."[3]

Abba Antony said, "Those who sit in solitude and are quiet have escaped from three wars: hearing, speaking, seeing: yet against one thing shall they continually battle: that is, their own heart.[4]

Abba Macarius the Elder used to say to the brothers in Scete, "When mass is ended in the church, flee, my brothers." And one of the brothers said to him, "Father, in this solitude where is there to flee further?" And he laid his finger upon his mouth saying, "This is what I would have you flee." And so he would go into his cell and shut the door and there sit alone.[5]

Abba Nilus said, "Invulnerable from the arrows of the enemy is the person who loves quiet: but the one who mixes with the crowd is often wounded."[6]

Abba Macarius said to the Abba Arsenius, "Why do you flee from us?" And the old man said, "God knows that I love you: but I cannot be with God and with people. A thousand and a thousand thousand of the angelic powers have one will: and people have many. Wherefore I cannot send God from me and come and be with others."[7]

There are many who live in the mountains and behave as if they were in the town, and they are wasting their time. It is possible to be a solitary in one's mind while living in a crowd, and it is possible for one who is a solitary to live in the crowd of his or her own thoughts.[8]

Amma Syncletica

A certain brother who lived solitary was disturbed in mind and making his way to Abba Theodore of Pherme he told him that he was troubled. The old man said to him, "Go, humble your spirit and submit yourself, and live with others." So he went away to the mountain, and dwelt with others. And afterwards he came back to the old man and said to him, "I have not found peace living with others." And the old man said, "If you cannot be at peace in solitude, nor yet with others, why did you want to be a monk? Was it not that you should have tribulation? Tell me now, how many years have you been wearing the monk's habit?" And the brother said, "Eight." And the old man said, "Believe me, I have been in this habit seventy years, and not for one day could I find peace: and you would have peace in eight?"⁹

Time with God

The kind of complete solitude sought by the desert saints may strike us as one of the strangest aspects of their life. We easily understand community and concerted effort made with others, but to choose to spend most of your life on your own? Antony says that the monk, away from solitude, is like a fish out of water. We may think that the reverse is true of us. What do you feel like when you are alone for long periods of time? Do you feel that it is an unnatural state, a waiting-to-be-with-others? Do you only "feel yourself" when surrounded by friends and family? Loneliness and solitude really have very little to do with each other.

We do not usually choose to be lonely; it is something that makes us uncomfortable. With loneliness comes the sense of not being valued, of being "left out" of what other people are enjoying. The desert saints chose solitude for very definite reasons. They were at peace with their solitude because essentially they were not alone. Their solitude placed them continually in the presence of God.

Often our first memories are social memories of our parents or playmates. Our development as a person seems to have been in the context of different relationships: children, school friends, colleagues, and partners. We may feel that only society, or more particularly, the close "defining" relationships we have had, can allow us to know who we really are. Separation from that web of relationships where we know and are known could perhaps strike us as a scary experience. We might only feel happy answering the question "Who am I?" in purely social terms. The desert saints would say that such an answer would be incomplete. If they had experienced the crowded and hectic lives we tend to live today, they might have doubted whether we could ever answer the question "Who am I?" From their point of view, before we are anything else, we are God's children; and each one of us is a unique creation.

The person that God created you to be may not be obvious. You may catch sight of who you are from time to time, just as when you see your face reflected clearly in a pool of water before the restless ripples sweep over the surface again. Perhaps, in truth, we have barely glimpsed the person God intended us to be. When we grow tired of the fickleness and constant change of the world, perhaps then we begin to understand why the desert saints set so much value on their solitude. The Christian life is about becoming the persons we were created to be. That may sound strange, but so much of our life is like the bubbles and ripples on the surface of a body of water.

Solitude is not just a bit of peace and quiet, it is a commitment to finding out who we really are. That this is a serious commitment is revealed by the story of the brother who gets into trouble for trying to be a solitary all at once. He was "trying to run before he could walk" in the ascetic life. The others seem harsh with him, but they are motivated by love. The benefits of solitude would be lost forever if they were treated as just another worldly achievement about which we could boast. The desert saints evidently saw solitude as something a person "grew into," an indicator of spiritual maturity. Why should this be? Because as we receive from God a clearer view of who we really are, the spiritual struggles become more intense. As Antony said, the wars of hearing, speaking, and seeing give way to the greatest field of conflict, the battle of the heart. Our recovery from the effects of sin is like a long convalescence from an illness that was almost fatal. We need patience, great commitment, and a steady openness to the mercy of God.

The fact that the great figures of the Old Testament (Abraham, Moses, Elijah, Jacob, and David) received so much from God in times of solitude would not have been lost on the desert saints. Solitude is the place both of wrestling with God and breaking through into new understanding (just like Jacob's wrestling with the angel [Genesis 32:22-29]). Elijah, when he most needed to receive guidance from God, was led further and further into the wilderness of solitude and there heard God's "still small voice" (1 Kings 19:4-18; RSV). One cannot help but think that the "still small voice" that speaks in each of us is too often drowned out by the uproar of our lives in the world.

You might feel, at this stage, a little gloomy about the prospects of ever attaining the kind of solitude achieved by the desert saints. Your life may be full of competing demands on your time and energy. These demands may also be perfectly reasonable and natural. You have a career to pursue, or you are married and need to spend time with your partner. You may have children and the God-given responsibility of caring for them. These are not trivial things by any means; but they may leave you too tired, too distracted, or too involved to think about solitude. Here the pattern of life Jesus had with his disciples is very helpful. It is a pattern of advance and retreat. There were the journeys all around Israel and even over the borders into neighboring countries that brought activity, conflict, and the hustle of crowds. But there were also the regular times of retreat into the desert when they could rest together. "Come away to a deserted place all by yourselves and rest a while," said Jesus to the disciples (Mark 6:31). There is a rhythm here that we do well to reflect upon. Is your life all advance with hardly any retreat? If Christ and the disciples needed time to draw back from the world, shouldn't you also make time for this? How can you make this happen?

Solitude is obviously intended to be far more than just being physically alone. It is the way we form a habit of retreat, creating a space and a time when God can speak to us. Perhaps you are fortunate enough to have some place in your house that could become a place of retreat. Some people have a favorite walk that becomes a "prayer walk." Every large city, despite the noise and crowds, has places of great solitude and peace. Often city center churches are examples of this. What is certain is that if we create a place where we can regularly turn to God, he will meet us there. There, as Amma Syncletica said, "it is possible to be a solitary in one's mind while living in a crowd." Time spent with God in solitude will always bring a harvest. The problems we leave outside the solitude will seem different when we return to them refreshed and strengthened. The surer sense of our relationship with Christ that solitude brings spills over into everything else we do. When Moses came down from his solitude on Mount Sinai, his face shone (Exodus 34:29-35). For you, too, solitude can be a place of transfiguration, a meeting place with the living God.

For Reflection

- What do you think is the difference between being alone and being lonely? Think of a time when you have needed to seek solitude. What drove you to be by yourself? Did it help? If so, how?
- Jesus frequently took his disciples into the desert to rest and recuperate; do you have a similar rhythm in your Christian life? Should you?
- Some people appear to have a vocation to the solitary life. What do you think God is saying to the church through their lives? What contribution do they make to the world?
- We spend so much time with others, willingly and unwillingly. Are we just a little uncomfortable in our own company? Do we reach for the nearest distraction rather than accepting and learning from our solitude? What difference could solitude make in your life?

Meditation on Solitude

My hope is in the Father,
my refuge is the Son,
my shelter is the Holy Spirit.

O Holy Trinity,
Glory to Thee.
Glory to the Father, and to the Son,
and to the Holy Spirit,
both now, and ever
and unto ages of ages.
Amen.

Elijah the prophet traveled
many days into solitude
and heard, Lord, your
still small voice.
Wrapped in the mantle
of our own solitude
may we hear
your voice in our hearts.

Let our times alone
with you be like
the waiting seed in the earth
promising Spring.

Holy God
Holy Mighty
Holy Immortal
have mercy upon us.

My hope is in the Father,
my refuge is the Son,
my shelter is the Holy Spirit.

Amen.

Endurance

Chapter Eight

ENDURANCE

When the wind blows steadily, sailors can think highly of themselves and boast of their skill; but only a sudden change of wind reveals the skill of the experienced helmsmen.[1]

Abba Antony

Faith consists not only in being baptised into Christ, but in fulfilling his commandments. Holy baptism is perfect and offers us perfection, but does not perfect a person who fails to fulfill the commandments.[2]

Mark the Ascetic

In the beginning there are a great many battles and a good deal of suffering for those who are advancing towards God and afterwards, ineffable joy. It is like those who wish to light a fire; at first they are choked by the smoke and cry, and by this means obtain what they seek...: so we must kindle the divine fire in ourselves through tears and hard work.[3]

Amma Syncletica

Abba Isaiah said, "Nothing is so useful to the beginner as insults. The beginner who bears insults is like a tree that is watered every day."[4]

Of our own will we remain there where our love is, even if we have been baptised, for the freedom of our will is not constrained. When the Scriptures say that "the kingdom of heaven suffers violence"...they are speaking of one's own will, so that each one of us should urge ourself, after baptism, not to turn towards evil but to abide in good.[5]

Mark the Ascetic

An old man was asked, "Why are we thus warred against by the demons?" He said, "Because we have cast away our arms; I mean, contempt of honors, humility, poverty, and endurance."[6]

A certain brother asked the abbot Poemen, saying, "What am I to do, Father, for I am troubled by sadness?" The old man said to him, "Look to no one for anything, condemn no one, disparage no one and God shall give you rest."[7]

A brother questioned an old man, "Tell me something which I can do, so that I may live by it," and the old man said, "If you can bear to be despised, that is a great thing, more than all the other virtues."[8]

There were two monks living in one place, and a great old man came to visit them with the intention of testing them. He took a stick and began to bang about the vegetables of one of them. Seeing it, the brother hid himself, and when only one shoot was left, he said to the old man, "Abba, if you will, leave it so that I can cook it that we may eat together." Then the old man bowed in penitence to the brother, saying, "Because of your long-suffering, the Holy Spirit rests on you, brother."[9]

Abba Antony said, "A time is coming when people will go mad, and when they see those who are not mad, they will attack them saying, 'You are mad, you are not like us.'"[10]

Holy Stubbornness

We live in a society that demands quick results and easy success. If something does not seem to work the first time, we try something else. Sometimes we just want change for change's sake—out with the old, in with the new! The same can be true of our attitude to faith; we can often be too impatient, expecting to go by leaps and bounds into the kingdom of God without very much effort. We forget, at these moments, the nature of Christ's invitation and his warning, "Enter through the narrow gate; for the gate is wide and the road is easy that leads to destruction, and there are many who take it. For the gate is narrow and the road is hard that leads to life, and there are few who find it" (Matthew 7:13-14).

Perhaps we have felt some excitement in serving God, some sign of the Holy Spirit at work around us. Perhaps we have felt drawn close to God in prayer. Do we then think that we shall always experience these things? Will the Christian life, for us, be always smooth sailing? "When the wind blows steadily," says the wise Antony, "sailors can think highly of themselves and boast of their skill; but only a sudden change of wind reveals the skill of the experienced helmsmen." When we encounter difficulty and obstacles, when it is no longer quite so exciting to be a Christian, our faith may falter. That is when the virtues of endurance are an essential part of the spiritual life.

The desert saints lived in an age when active persecution was a reality for the whole church. The stories of the first Christian martyrs were still very fresh in their minds. Indeed, in Antony's lifetime there was a great persecution in Alexandria during which he assisted the church and appeared fearlessly in public, facing great danger. The desert saints knew that their decision to follow Christ could cost them everything. Parts of the Christian communion of today still have to endure persecution even to death. However, away from the great dramas of witnessing to the faith with one's life, there are the lesser martyrdoms that come the way of every Christian. Two of the sayings in this chapter are about being despised and insulted. We may find that we are laughed at for our faith. Since we are social beings, this can be painful. Sometimes people will think that we are rather odd for taking our faith so seriously. Antony speaks very clearly to the spirit of our own age when he says, "People will go mad, and when they see those who are not mad, they will attack them saying, 'You are mad, you are not like us.'" Being a Christian may well put us out of step with the people around us, yet the saints see this as a way by which the strength of our devotion to Christ can be proved. Abba Isaiah says, "The beginner who bears insults is like a tree that is watered every day."

However, coping with ridicule is only a small part of the way our faith can be proved, as gold is proved in refining fires (1 Peter 1:6-7). Periods of adversity or tragedy, when the world gets rough, are times when our belief in a wise, all-powerful, and loving God is put under a great deal of strain. We may not understand what is happening to us or to those we love. Sometimes Christians have to become like Job, trusting God against the advice of friends, trusting him in the midst of desolation. These are moments when the stiff breeze of Antony's image blows up into a storm.

We are also required to endure our own fallibility and weakness. We feel, perhaps, that we are making progress; then things suddenly fall apart. Perhaps some old sin makes its appearance, perhaps temptation gets the better of us and we feel ashamed and disheartened. The temptation to feeling disheartened, even lapsing into outright despair about what we imagine to be "our hopeless case," was well known to the desert saints. They were not superhuman; their rule of life took it for granted that they would frequently fall away from the narrow path they had set themselves. A monk, when asked about his rule, replied that it consisted of "falling down and getting up." It is the getting up that counts, not giving up on ourselves because we can be sure that God never gives up on us.

Amma Syncletica's comment about the nature of discipleship is very helpful. She speaks of battles and suffering and the need to persevere, but she also speaks of ineffable joy. We must not feel that something is wrong when we enter these times of testing. We should instead think of them as moments when God asks us to show our love for him.

Endurance can be characterized as a certain "holy stubbornness." When we hit trouble, this stubbornness enables us to trust God's love and to continue to plow the furrow we have been given to plow (Luke 9:62). There must have been many moments in the decades that the saints spent in the desert when they wondered whether they had chosen to do the right thing with their lives. Many of them had given up a good deal for the solitude of their cells. It would be only human to reflect on the family and children they would never have. At those times, their "holy stubbornness" and obedience must have been of tremendous value.

However, the desert saints' endurance was not pursued for selfish ends. They saw their ascetic lives as a sign to the whole world. By virtue of their extraordinary efforts to achieve stillness and purity of heart, they became an immense resource to the people of their own time. The very fact that we are now reflecting on their teaching the best part of two thousand years later is the real indicator of what fruit that endurance produced. The desert saints have risen to the promise of Jesus in John's Gospel, "You did not choose me but I chose you. And I appointed you to go and bear fruit, *fruit that will last*" (John 15:16).

If we, too, are to bear fruit that will last, then endurance in our faith must be our common task today. We have a profound responsibility by virtue of the Lord's command to make disciples of all nations (Matthew 28:19), not just to disappear within the church where we can be with fellow Christians, but to present Christ to the world through the medium of every Christian life. In whatever part of our lives, whether public or private, at work or at home, we live for the Lord whose Spirit rests upon us. Mark the Ascetic makes the nature of the task clear when he says of baptism, "Holy baptism is perfect and offers us perfection, but does not perfect the person who fails to fulfill the commandments." Baptism is just the beginning of a journey with God. True, the journey would not be possible without baptism; but if we do not endure in our faith, neither will it guarantee our fullest development as both a Christian and a human being. What is set before us is the awesome prospect of attaining "to the measure of the full stature of Christ" (Ephesians 4:13).

This would be an impossible task for any human being were it not for the fact that we worship a God who keeps his promises. The yoke we have to bear is, through his love and mercy, an easy one (Matthew 11:29-30). Even though the path of discipleship is utterly demanding, the alternatives to enduring in our faith are not real alternatives. Apart from God there is nothing good, nothing of value. He is the source of our very lives, our Father and Creator. We have been called out of darkness into his marvelous light. Through grace we shall live in that light forever.

For Reflection

- The desert saints took it for granted that their faith would bring conflict and opposition. Does this seem strange to you? Have you ever experienced conflict with others because of your faith? If so, how? How much mockery and embarrassment are you willing to bear through standing up for your beliefs?
- Many people dedicate a tremendous amount of their time and energy to sports and hobbies. Does it seem strange to you that the same qualities of commitment and perseverance are not often dedicated to knowing God?

- The Christian's relationship to the world has been described as being that of "a stranger and pilgrim." Would you see yourself in these terms? Explain.
- What do you make of the idea of "holy stubbornness"? Are there areas in your life where you have had to make a stand regarding some aspect of your Christian beliefs?

Meditation on Endurance

My hope is in the Father,
my refuge is the Son,
my shelter is the Holy Spirit.

O Holy Trinity,
Glory to Thee.
Glory to the Father, and to the Son,
and to the Holy Spirit,
both now, and ever
and unto ages of ages.
Amen.

As a sail luffs to contrary winds
so our will to follow you
shifts and changes.
O Lord who never changes
steady our course in the storms of life.

As the fire's embers blow
hot and cold, even so
our love fades
even to the edge of darkness.

O rushing Holy Spirit
fan even our dull hearts,
chilled by sin, to flame.

Holy God
Holy Mighty
Holy Immortal
have mercy upon us.

My hope is in the Father,
my refuge is the Son,
my shelter is the Holy Spirit.

Amen.

Coptic Cartouche

GUIDANCE FOR GROUP FACILITATORS

Setting

The sessions of this encounter with the desert saints need not take place in church. All that is required is a room that is large enough for people to find their own space to be slightly apart from their fellow participants for the earlier parts of each session. Ideally, it would be a quiet room where people can easily feel relaxed. Try hard to avoid the atmosphere of the schoolroom or seminar! I suggest that an icon be placed somewhere in the room, preferably one of Christ or of the Holy Trinity, with a small candle burning before it. The sessions are designed to last for about an hour.

Conduct of Sessions

If possible, distribute copies of the book before the day of the first session so that people can read "Introduction to the Desert Saints" and "Monastic Egypt" (pages 9–13) and set what they are about to experience in a historical context. This prevents such preliminary questions taking over the subject of the first session itself. In my experience, this study works best in a small group setting of no more than twelve persons.

Hesychia, variously translated silence or stillness, was a tremendously important part of the desert spirituality, something we find very hard to achieve in our own day. I suggest the sessions start very simply in silent prayer with the people sitting together in a rough circle with the icon and candle as a focus for the eye. After a time, use a few of the sentences provided for focus (see pages 89–91), with silence between, and conclude with a quiet saying of the Lord's Prayer.

Then ask participants to go apart on their own to read and reflect on the quotations that begin the chapter you are covering in that session. There may well be the tendency to "rattle through" the quotations rather superficially. The approach we are trying to achieve is akin to the way one would drink a truly rich, delicious beverage in contrast to the way one would drink ordinary water. Please urge the participants to mull over the sayings, allowing a deeper response to the images, thoughts, or memories that arise in their mind. Encourage participants to make their own notes, even to draw pictures as they occur to them. Emphasize that these notes need not be seen by anyone else, so there is no pressure to produce something "respectable." This should take around fifteen-to-twenty minutes.

When people feel they have a fairly complete initial response to the quotations, ask them to form groups of two or three persons. As the facilitator, be fairly active in the make-up of these groups because how these groups are formed will affect enormously the quality of the work done in them. Think very hard beforehand how to achieve a good balance in the group. Try to avoid clutches of bosom pals, relatives, extroverts, introverts, and so on. Then have the small groups reflect on the questions that follow in each chapter. There is no obligation upon the people in each group to reach consensus regarding what the sayings are "about." There may not even be many discernible "answers," although participants may see certain themes or principles emerging. What is important is the exploration of the ideas with others, who act as a resource each to the other. Allow an additional fifteen minutes or so for this.

Then bring everyone back into the single large group. Do not ask the smaller groups to report everything they have discussed or thought. Too much talking at this stage could be very unhelpful. Rather, encourage individuals to relate in just a few words what they will take away from the session. For example, some theme or principle might have become clearer, some memory might have been revived, or some new light might have been cast on an incident in the Gospels. If, as the facilitator, you feel the need to draw things together at this stage, I suggest a very light touch. For it may well be that God will give quite different things to those who have taken part, which might only be destroyed by a set of forced conclusions. Do not be afraid to leave ideas hanging in the air.

The session can conclude with the meditation written especially for it and an appropriate blessing. The meditations include elements of ancient prayers from the Orthodox liturgy. The use of silence and repetition is to encourage a contemplative state of mind where we listen to God more than we speak.

Participants usually appreciate a bit of social time after each session. Those relatively unused to this kind of approach may need to "shift gears" before leaving.

PRAYERS AND SENTENCES

The supreme prayer of the desert saints and of later Eastern monasticism (apart, of course, from the Lord's Prayer) was the Jesus Prayer, which is found in its fullest form as follows:

Lord Jesus Christ,
Son of God,
have mercy upon me,
a sinner.

This is always addressed afresh to Christ as a genuine prayer and should never become a mere formula or mantra. During silent prayer it can serve to focus the thoughts and redirect the heart to God when it has drifted off in distractions. Another prayer also used in the meditations at the conclusion of each session is the Trisagion (literally, the Thrice Holy):

Holy God,
Holy Mighty,
Holy Immortal,
have mercy upon us.

With these prayers, simplicity is the keynote. Let silence do its work. Think of the prayers as touches on the rudder during an otherwise silent voyage.

Sentences

These sentences are from the Psalms, which were the daily meditation of the desert saints:

You show me the path of life.
In your presence there is fullness of joy;
in your right hand are pleasures forevermore.
(Psalm 16:11)

I call upon the LORD,
who is worthy to be praised,
so I shall be saved from my enemies.
(Psalm 18:3)

The law of the LORD is perfect,
reviving the soul;
the decrees of the LORD are sure,
making wise the simple.
(Psalm 19:7)

Make me to know your ways, O LORD;
teach me your paths.
Lead me in your truth, and teach me,
for you are the God of my salvation.
(Psalm 25:4-5a)

Into your hand I commit my spirit;
you have redeemed me,
O LORD, faithful God.
(Psalm 31:5)

Our soul waits for the LORD;
   he is our help and shield.
               (Psalm 33:20)

For with you is the fountain of life;
   in your light we see light.
               (Psalm 36:9)

Take delight in the LORD,
   and he will give you the
   desires of your heart.
               (Psalm 37:4)

Whom have I in heaven but you?
And there is nothing on earth
   that I desire other than you.
               (Psalm 73:25)

NOTES

Charity

1. *The Sayings of the Desert Fathers: The Alphabetical Collection*, translated by Benedicta Ward (Oxford: Mowbray [now Cassells], 1975, 1981), p. 3.
2. Ibid., p. 230.
3. *The Wisdom of the Desert Fathers*, translated by Benedicta Ward (Oxford: SLG Press, 1975, 1981), p. 42.
4. Ibid., p. 61.
5. Ibid., pp. 61–62.
6. Ibid., p. 48
7. Ibid., p. 49.
8. *The Desert Fathers*, translated by Helen Waddell (London: Constable & Co., 1987), p. 204.
9. *The Sayings of the Desert Fathers: The Alphabetical Collection*, p. 42.
10. Ibid., p. 90.
11. Ibid., p. 150.

Temptation

1. *The Sayings of the Desert Fathers: The Alphabetical Collection*, translated by Benedicta Ward (Oxford: Mowbray [now Cassells], 1975, 1981), p. 84.
2. *Early Fathers from the Philokalia*, translated by E. Kadloubovsky and G.E.H. Palmer (London: Faber and Faber, 1954, 1981), p. 83.
3. Ibid., p. 110.
4. Ibid., p. 84.
5. Ibid., p. 114.
6. *The Wisdom of the Desert Fathers*, translated by Benedicta Ward (Oxford: SLG Press, 1975, 1981), p. 8.

7. Ibid., p. 23.

8. Ibid., p. 25.

9. *The Desert Fathers*, translated by Helen Waddell (London: Constable & Co., 1987), p. 144.

10. Ibid., p. 143.

Self-Control

1. *The Sayings of the Desert Fathers: The Alphabetical Collection*, translated by Benedicta Ward (Oxford: Mowbray [now Cassells], 1975, 1981), p. 187.

2. Ibid., p. 83.

3. *The Wisdom of the Desert Fathers*, translated by Benedicta Ward (Oxford: SLG Press, 1975, 1981), p. 37.

4. Ibid., p. 60.

5. *The Sayings of the Desert Fathers: The Alphabetical Collection*, p. 233.

6. *The Desert Fathers*, translated by Helen Waddell (London: Constable & Co., 1987), p. 104.

7. Ibid., p. 138.

8. *The Wisdom of the Desert Fathers*, p. 17.

9. Ibid., p. 48.

10. Ibid., p. 39.

Stillness

1. *The Philokalia: The Complete Text*, Volume 1, translated by E. Kadloubovsky and G.E.H. Palmer (London: Faber and Faber, 1979), pp. 31–32.

2. Ibid., p. 33.

3. *The Wisdom of the Desert Fathers*, translated by Benedicta Ward (Oxford: SLG Press, 1975, 1981), p. 1.

4. Ibid., p. 4.

5. *The Sayings of the Desert Fathers: The Alphabetical Collection*, translated by Benedicta Ward (Oxford: Mowbray [now Cassells], 1975, 1981), p. 178.

6. Ibid., p. 220.

7. Ibid., p. 22.

8. Ibid., p. 171.

9. *The Wisdom of the Desert Fathers*, p. 33.

10. *The Philokalia: The Complete Text*, Volume 1, p. 35.

Prayer

1. *The Desert Fathers*, translated by Helen Waddell (London: Constable & Co., 1987), p. 157.

2. Ibid., p. 159.

3. *Early Fathers from the Philokalia*, translated by E. Kadloubovsky and G.E.H. Palmer (London: Faber and Faber, 1954, 1981), p. 130.

4. Ibid., p. 130.

5. Ibid., p. 131.

6. Ibid., p. 133.

7. *The Philokalia: The Complete Text*, Volume 1, translated by E. Kadloubovsky and G.E.H. Palmer (London: Faber and Faber, 1979), p. 118.

8. *Early Fathers from the Philokalia*, p. 133.

9. Ibid., p. 135.

10. *The Sayings of the Desert Fathers: The Alphabetical Collection*, translated by Benedicta Ward (Oxford: Mowbray [now Cassells], 1975, 1981), p. 3.

11. *The Philokalia: The Complete Text*, Volume 1, p. 112.

Simplicity

1. *The Sayings of the Desert Fathers: The Alphabetical Collection*, translated by Benedicta Ward (Oxford: Mowbray [now Cassells], 1975, 1981), p. 16.

2. *The Desert Fathers*, translated by Helen Waddell (London: Constable & Co., 1987), p. 172.

3. Ibid., p. 121.

4. Ibid., pp. 121–22.

5. *The Sayings of the Desert Fathers: The Alphabetical Collection*, p. 2.

6. Ibid., p. 197.

7. Ibid., p. 236.

8. Ibid., p. 183.

9. Ibid., p. 233.

10. *Early Fathers from the Philokalia*, translated by E. Kadloubovsky and G.E.H. Palmer (London: Faber and Faber, 1954, 1981), p. 22.

11. *The Sayings of the Desert Fathers: The Alphabetical Collection*, p. 70.

Solitude

1. *The Desert Fathers*, translated by Helen Waddell (London: Constable & Co., 1987), p. 91.

2. Ibid., p. 133.

3. Ibid., pp. 149–50.

4. Ibid., p. 91.

5. Ibid., p. 102.

6. Ibid., p. 94.

7. Ibid., p. 175.

8. *The Sayings of the Desert Fathers: The Alphabetical Collection*, translated by Benedicta Ward (Oxford: Mowbray [now Cassells], 1975, 1981), p. 234.

9. *The Desert Fathers*, p. 123.

Endurance

1. *Early Fathers from the Philokalia*, translated by E. Kadloubovsky and G.E.H. Palmer (London: Faber and Faber, 1954, 1981), p. 43.

2. Ibid., p. 63.

3. *The Sayings of the Desert Fathers: The Alphabetical Collection*, translated by Benedicta Ward (Oxford: Mowbray [now Cassells], 1975, 1981), pp. 230–31.

4. Ibid., p. 69.

5. *Early Fathers from the Philokalia*, p. 63.

6. *The Wisdom of the Desert Fathers*, translated by Benedicta Ward (Oxford: SLG Press, 1975, 1981), p. 48.

7. *The Desert Fathers*, translated by Helen Waddell (London: Constable & Co., 1987), p. 202.

8. *The Wisdom of the Desert Fathers*, translated by Benedicta Ward (Oxford: SLG Press, 1975, 1981), p. 52.

9. Ibid., pp. 57–58.

10. *The Sayings of the Desert Fathers: The Alphabetical Collection*, p. 6.

BIBLIOGRAPHY

The Desert Fathers, translated by Helen Waddell (London: Constable & Co., 1987).

Early Fathers from the Philokalia, translated by E. Kadloubovsky and G.E.H. Palmer (London: Faber and Faber, 1954, 1981).

The Philokalia: The Complete Text, Volume 1, translated by E. Kadloubovsky and G.E.H. Palmer (London: Faber and Faber, 1979).

The Sayings of the Desert Fathers: The Alphabetical Collection, translated by Benedicta Ward (Oxford: Mowbray [now Cassells], 1975, 1981).

The Wisdom of the Desert Fathers, translated by Benedicta Ward (Oxford: SLG Press, 1975, 1981).

FURTHER READING

Bondi, Roberta. *To Love as God Loves: Conversations with the Early Church*. Minneapolis: Fortress Press, 1987.

———. *To Pray and to Love: Conversations on Prayer with the Desert Fathers*. Minneapolis: Fortress Press, 1991.

Chitty, Derwas James. *The Desert a City: An Introduction to the Study of Egyptian and Palestian Monasticism Under the Christian Empire*. Crestwood, New York: St. Vladimir's Seminary Press, 1977.

Kadloubovsky, E., and Palmer, G. E. H., trans. *Writings from the Philokalia on Prayer of the Heart*. London: Faber & Faber, 1951. Reprinted in 1992.

Kallistos Ware, Bishop. *The Power of the Name*. Oxford: SLG Press, 1974.

Merton, Thomas. *Wisdom of the Desert*. W. W. Norton & Company, 1988.

Waddell, H. *The Desert Fathers*. London: Constable & Co, 1936.

Ward, Benedicta, and Norman Russell. *Lives of the Desert Fathers: The Historia Monachorum in Aegypto* (Cistercian Studies No. 34). Oxford: Mowbray, 1981.

Ward, Benedicta, trans. *The Sayings of the Desert Fathers: The Alphabetical Collection*. Oxford: Mowbray, 1981.